**Vocabulary Tests
Level 1**

Suitable for ages 7 – 9

Each word study unit contains

- Definition matching
- Cloze sentences

Contents

Unit 1	page 2
Unit 2	page 4
Unit 3	page 6
Unit 4	page 8
Unit 5	page 10
Unit 6	page 12
Unit 7	page 14
Unit 8	page 16
Unit 9	page 18
Unit 10	page 20
Test 1	page 22
Test 2	page 26
Test 3	page 30
Test 4	page 34
Test 5	page 38

Solutions

Unit 1	page 42
Unit 2	page 42
Unit 3	page 42
Unit 4	page 43
Unit 5	page 43
Unit 6	page 44
Unit 7	page 44
Unit 8	page 44
Unit 9	page 45
Unit 10	page 45
Test 1	page 46
Test 2	page 47
Test 3	page 48
Test 4	page 49
Test 5	page 50

Copyright © 2017 Simon Steggels
All rights reserved

No part of this book may be reproduced, stored in a retrieval system, communicated or transmitted in any form or by any means without prior written permission. All inquiries should be made to the publisher.

ISBN 978-0-6480967-5-7

Published by
Advanced Instruction Pty Ltd
www.advancedinstruction.com.au

Unit 1

Definitions—match the words in the bold with their meanings below

servant	**mountain**	**plenty**	**noun**
during	**worry**	**energy**	**adjective**
unpack	**greedy**	**exciting**	**verb**
fireplace	**leak**	**famous**	**adverb**

1. someone whose job is to cook, clean or do other work in someone else's home _____
2. a very big hill much higher than the land around it _____
3. a place in a room where an open fire burns for heat or cooking _____
4. to be nervous and upset _____
5. to take things out of a suitcase, especially clothes _____
6. the power you have for doing things that need effort _____
7. from the beginning to the end; while _____
8. a word that refers to a person, place or thing _____
9. wanting more money, power, food, things than you need _____
10. water or liquid flowing out of a container _____
11. a word that refers to doing, being or having _____
12. more than enough _____
13. a word that adds more information to a verb—how, when, where, how much _____
14. a word that adds more information to a noun—describing _____
15. interesting and full of action _____
16. someone or something that is very well known _____

Unit 1

Word usage—complete the sentences using the words in bold from the previous page

1. The word *pencil* is a _____ and so are *shop* and *weekday*.

2. Don't worry; we have _____ of time to get to the train station.

3. The word *run* is a _____ and so are *own* and *taste*.

4. Most people work _____ the day and sleep at night.

5. 'Pick up your own clothes,' said Mum. 'I am not your _____.'

6. The Sydney Opera House is Australia's most _____ building.

7. The word *quickly* is an _____ and so are *too* and *very*.

8. 'Don't be so _____!' my mother told me. 'Those lollies are for everyone at the party to share.'

9. As soon as we get to the hotel, I will _____ my bags and then go for a swim.

10. In winter, some people use a _____ to heat their homes.

11. Don't _____ about your test tomorrow because you have studied hard.

12. There is a _____ in the watering can you are carrying.

13. We left early in the morning for our hike up the _____.

14. The word *tiny* is an _____ and so are *hot* and *perfect*.

15. After the cross-country race, I had no _____ left at all.

16. It was very _____ to ride the waterslides at Wet World.

© MR STEGGELS ADVANCED INSTRUCTION PTY LTD

Unit 2

Definitions—match the words in the bold with their meanings below

snug	machine	rhyme	whole
busy	**handle**	**paragraph**	**sentence**
peep	**batteries**	**describe**	**character**
extra	**beautiful**	**clever**	**correctly**

1. having the same last sound; a short poem for children _____

2. a secret, quick look _____

3. to say or write what something or someone is like _____

4. warm, comfortable and protected _____

5. these make electricity for toys, radios, cars _____

6. a lot of things to do; full of activity _____

7. a short piece of writing with at least one sentence, and that begins on a new line _____

8. grab onto this to hold, move or carry something _____

9. learns and understands things quickly and easily _____

10. something more, added to what is normal _____

11. complete; altogether _____

12. something with moving parts that uses power to do a job _____

13. a group of words that starts with a capital letter _____

14. very pretty, pleasant, kind _____

15. done or answered the right way _____

16. a person in a film, play or book _____

Unit 2

Word usage—complete the sentences using the words in bold from the previous page

1. If you need _____ help with your work, please raise your hand.

2. We spent the _____ day cleaning out the garage.

3. I turned the door _____ but it was locked and I couldn't get out.

4. He is _____ at mathematics and can solve most problems quickly.

5. We were _____ in the kitchen, making cupcakes for my birthday party.

6. *Baa, Baa, Black sheep* is an example of a famous nursery _____.

7. I saw my brother _____ through the curtains at the Christmas tree.

8. In this story, the main _____ has to find the *Lost City of Gold*.

9. We had _____ weather on our recent trip to the Gold Coast.

10. Your _____ must end with a full stop.

11. I curled up in bed, all _____ and cosy while the wind shook my window.

12. The _____ in my remote control car have gone flat.

13. In our writing lesson, we had to _____ a photograph in detail.

14. I won the quiz by answering the final question _____.

15. My teacher asked us to leave a line between each new _____.

16. I put the dirty clothes into the washing _____.

Unit 3

Definitions—match the words in the bold with their meanings below

carry	different	island	common
collect	special	scared	whisper
underneath	strike	interesting	germs
upright	control	discovered	favourite

1. not ordinary or usual _____

2. a piece of land surrounded by water _____

3. found _____

4. frightened or worried _____

5. to get and keep something _____

6. to hit or attack _____

7. below _____

8. something that gets your attention, making you want to know more about it _____

9. straight up _____

10. to speak very quietly _____

11. not the same _____

12. order, limit or rule people or actions _____

13. the same in a lot of places for many people _____

14. very small things that cause people to get sick _____

15. to hold onto something and move it from one place to another _____

16. liked best or most enjoyed _____

© MR STEGGELS ADVANCED INSTRUCTION PTY LTD

Unit 3

Word usage—complete the sentences using the words in bold from the previous page

1. This story is not very _____ because nothing much happens.

2. I searched for my missing shirt and finally _____ it at the bottom of the basket of washing.

3. I have to _____ my heavy bag to and from softball training.

4. It is _____ to see twins dressed in the same clothes.

5. I wanted to go on the rollercoaster but my friend was too _____ .

6. I found my favourite toy _____ my bed.

7. My brother could not _____ his joy when he saw his birthday presents.

8. Australia is an _____; it is completely surrounded by water.

9. Sit _____ in your chair so you don't hurt your back.

10. A wedding is a very _____ event.

11. My teacher asked me to _____ the lunch orders from the canteen.

12. In soccer, you can only _____ the ball with your foot.

13. There are many _____ flavours of ice cream but I like vanilla best.

14. My _____ colour is blue. What is yours?

15. He leaned close to _____ in my ear so only I could hear.

16. To remove _____, always wash your hands with soap.

© MR STEGGELS ADVANCED INSTRUCTION PTY LTD

Unit 4

Definitions—match the words in the bold with their meanings below

happened	fetch	swap	upside down
plastic	date	huff	object
admit	trick	giggle	tickled
oval	imagine	either	bruise

1. to go get something or someone and bring it back _____

2. give something and get something else back; trade _____

3. material that can be bent into many different shapes, for different uses such as containers _____

4. to have an idea of something _____

5. a joke that fools or cheats someone; to fool or play a joke on someone _____

6. took place; had an effect on someone or something _____

7. also, too; one or the other _____

8. a day in a month and year _____

9. shaped like an egg; an area on which sport is played _____

10. the part that was at the bottom is now at the top _____

11. to laugh at something silly or rude or when you are nervous _____

12. a thing that you can see and touch but is not alive _____

13. agree with something that is true _____

14. a mark where the skin is darker in colour because blood is trapped there _____

15. touched someone lightly to make them laugh _____

16. angry and upset mood; bad temper _____

Unit 4

Word usage—complete the sentences using the words in bold from the previous page

1. The _____ of the surprise birthday party is the first of July.

2. The rollercoaster went _____ through the loop.

3. If I throw a stick, my dog will always _____ it.

4. We saw a strange _____ in the sky that seemed to be stopped in mid air.

5. I don't like to go outside when it's cold and my sister doesn't _____ .

6. The flowers were not real; they were made from _____ .

7. The table in the dining room is _____ in shape.

8. Try to _____ that you are a bird flying over the ocean.

9. When Dad stepped in a deep puddle and got angry, we all started to _____ .

10. He begged me to _____ my lunch for his, but I said that I didn't want to.

11. 'Go on, _____ that you stole my diary!' cried my sister.

12. Does anybody know what _____ to the last piece of chocolate cake?

13. My brother went off in a _____ because I beat him in a game of cards.

14. I had a purple _____ where the softball had hit my shoulder.

15. He _____ my feet to make me laugh.

16. I have been practising a magic _____ where I make a coin disappear.

© MR STEGGELS ADVANCED INSTRUCTION PTY LTD

Unit 5

Definitions—match the words in the bold with their meanings below

false	**event**	**pleased**	**anywhere**
properly	**reply**	**patient**	**program**
load	**arrow**	**explain**	**error**
though	**weren't**	**argue**	**caught**

1. when you do not agree with someone; to give reasons for what you think or believe _____

2. not true _____

3. but; as if _____

4. to answer _____

5. discovered doing something wrong _____

6. make something easy to understand _____

7. when you wait without complaining _____

8. done in the right way _____

9. were not _____

10. the amount of weight carried; to put a lot of things into something _____

11. in, to or at any place _____

12. a long, thin stick with a sharp point on one end and small feathers on the other _____

13. a mistake _____

14. instructions that are put into a computer to make it work _____

15. happy or satisfied _____

16. something important or unusual that happens _____

Unit 5

Word usage—complete the sentences using the words in bold from the previous page

1. You have to be _____ while you wait in line to see the teacher.

2. Mum told me not to _____ and to clean up my room right away.

3. Many people use a computer _____ that corrects their spelling.

4. I had to do my work again because I had not done it _____.

5. The high jump is my favourite _____ at the Olympics.

6. I circled _____ for question six, but the correct answer was *True*.

7. I skied the downhill course without a single _____.

8. We had to _____ to Mum how the kitchen got covered with flour.

9. Because it was raining, we _____ able to go for a walk along the beach.

10. I helped to _____ the car with gear for our picnic.

11. Even _____ the book is better, I still enjoyed the movie, *Matilda*.

12. I can't find my house keys _____.

13. Police _____ the robber as she tried to escape onto the train.

14. He was _____ with his performance at the soccer tryouts.

15. I had to _____ to the invitation by sending a card in the mail.

16. At camp, we got to use a bow and _____ in the archery range.

© MR STEGGELS ADVANCED INSTRUCTION PTY LTD

Unit 6

Definitions—match the words in the bold with their meanings below

clump	daughter	rather	poem
invite	another	fault	guilty
quiet	brought	grin	biscuit
uniform	badge	surprise	attention

1. a mistake; you are to blame for something _____
2. a special set of clothes worn by people who belong to a group _____
3. instead of; you prefer one thing to another _____
4. a group of trees, flowers; a solid chunk of something _____
5. feeling bad that you have done something wrong _____
6. making very little noise _____
7. a piece of writing on separate lines sometimes ending with words that rhyme _____
8. one more person or thing or amount _____
9. to ask someone to an event _____
10. something not expected _____
11. wide smile _____
12. a female child _____
13. took or carried something or someone to a place _____
14. a small, flat disc of dry food that can be sweet or savoury _____
15. a small piece of metal or plastic worn to show who you are, what group you belong to, what you have achieved _____
16. notice taken of something _____

Unit 6

Word usage—complete the sentences using the words in bold from the previous page

1. We can't fit _____ person in our car as there are only five seats.

2. I got my football _____ off the clothesline and got dressed.

3. I wrote a _____ for my friend and printed it neatly inside a card.

4. Would you _____ go to see a movie or stay home and read a book?

5. It wasn't my _____ that the dog got out but I still got the blame.

6. Together, we pulled a large _____ of weeds out of the garden bed.

7. When the lights went off in our cabin, we had to be _____ and go to sleep.

8. When I fell over in the mud, my friend had a _____ on his face.

9. Did he _____ you to his birthday party?

10. Dad looked _____ when Mum asked who had taken the last cookie.

11. My parents have one _____ and one son.

12. I _____ my new puppy to school to show my classmates.

13. When I became a library monitor, I was given a special _____ to wear.

14. It was a _____ when I opened the front door and heard everyone shout, 'Happy birthday!'

15. I waved my arms in the air to get the _____ of the lifesavers.

16. He dipped the ginger _____ into his hot chocolate.

© MR STEGGELS ADVANCED INSTRUCTION PTY LTD

Unit 7

Definitions—match the words in the bold with their meanings below

instead	necklace	hardly	truly
forward	leader	earn	title
guessed	managed	besides	mystery
lean	pest	copied	wondered

1. a piece of jewellery worn around the neck _____
2. annoying person _____
3. attempted to give the right answer _____
4. in addition to; also _____
5. in place of something or someone else _____
6. get money for work done _____
7. arranged or did something; succeeded _____
8. used to show that you are honest in what you are saying _____
9. the person in charge of a group _____
10. the name of a book, film, song or similar _____
11. rest against; slope in one direction _____
12. thought about or wanted to know about something _____
13. something strange that cannot be explained _____
14. in the direction that is in front of you _____
15. made exactly the same as the very first one; moved something from one screen to another on a computer _____
16. only just _____

Unit 7

Word usage—complete the sentences using the words in bold from the previous page

1. We all agreed that Ralph should be the _____ of our hiking group.

2. There are no oranges left – would you like a banana _____ ?

3. She _____ to reach the finals of the sprint race.

4. Don't _____ on that old fence because it will fall over.

5. The boy was making a _____ of himself by asking too many questions.

6. I _____ correctly that there were 275 jellybeans in the jar.

7. Your writing is so small that I can _____ read it.

8. I enjoy reading about the _____ of the Lost City of Atlantis.

9. He didn't write the report himself – he _____ it from a website.

10. I _____ $5 each time I wash the car and weed the front garden.

11. A kangaroo hops in a _____ direction but cannot hop backwards.

12. The diamond _____ was stolen from the museum.

13. Have you ever _____ why the sky is blue?

14. Which flavour ice cream do you like, _____ strawberry?

15. A review should begin with the _____ and author of the book.

16. The haunted house ride was a _____ terrifying experience.

© MR STEGGELS ADVANCED INSTRUCTION PTY LTD

Unit 8

Definitions—match the words in the bold with their meanings below

rotten	stomp	clung	ever
picnic	bare	rough	realised
treat	jeans	arrived	pause
sole	gulp	trembling	again

1. shaking slightly because of fear, cold or being upset _____
2. a reward; a special experience _____
3. understood what was going on _____
4. smelly, very bad, not fresh _____
5. without any covering _____
6. held onto something tightly _____
7. a meal enjoyed outside _____
8. one more time _____
9. the bottom part of the foot or shoe that touches the ground _____
10. not smooth; uneven _____
11. to swallow a large amount or breathe in air quickly _____
12. walk with heavy steps especially when you are annoyed _____
13. reached a place at the end of a trip _____
14. at any time, since that time, in the same way as always _____
15. stop for a short period of time _____
16. pants made of strong, blue cotton _____

Unit 8

Word usage—complete the sentences using the words in bold from the previous page

1. I _____ that my answers were in the wrong order so I had to erase them.

2. It is not a good idea to walk the city streets in _____ feet.

3. The train _____ at the platform two minutes early.

4. The park by the river is a lovely place to have a _____ .

5. Whenever my teacher asks a question, there is always a _____ before someone raises a hand to answer.

6. The dirt road leading to the farm was very _____ and bumpy.

7. Have you _____ been to New York City?

8. As a _____ for all of our hard work, Dad bought us pizza.

9. Harry, our dog, likes to _____ down his food.

10. Don't _____ down the stairs – you'll wake the baby.

11. When I came out of the surf, I was _____ because the wind was so cold.

12. You don't have to dress up for my party; a t-shirt and _____ will be fine.

13. The new pre-school student _____ to his mother's dress.

14. She cut her _____ when she stepped on an oyster shell.

15. I added salt instead of sugar to my cake and had to start all over _____.

16. The rubbish bin is filled with _____ food and is attracting flies.

© MR STEGGELS ADVANCED INSTRUCTION PTY LTD

Unit 9

Definitions—match the words in the bold with their meanings below

launch	tour	twitch	howled
hinges	adjusted	further	gloom
collapse	haunted	knot	secure
laundry	hasty	dare	injured

1. pieces of metal that attach a door to the doorframe _____
2. a join made by tying together the ends of string, rope or cloth _____
3. a greater distance than before _____
4. to send a new ship into the water or a spacecraft into space _____
5. done in a hurry _____
6. changed something slightly to make it fit or work better _____
7. a short, sudden, jerky movement _____
8. a place to wash dirty clothes _____
9. made a long, loud, sad sound _____
10. a visit to a place to look around and learn about it _____
11. darkness that makes it difficult to see _____
12. describes a place where ghosts keep appearing _____
13. not likely to move or break _____
14. to ask someone to do something silly, embarrassing or dangerous _____
15. harmed _____
16. to fall down suddenly after losing strength or support _____

Unit 9

Word usage—complete the sentences using the words in bold from the previous page

1. The rain poured and the strong wind _____ in the trees.

2. There is a free _____ of the art gallery every day at 11 am.

3. When buying a new car, it is best not to make any _____ decisions.

4. The storm ripped the shed door off its _____ .

5. Those planks in the tree house don't look very _____ to me.

6. By age seven I was able to tie a _____ in my shoelaces.

7. I _____ you to pull a silly face in the class photograph.

8. The rocket will _____ in ten seconds.

9. My eyes were very tired from reading and they began to _____ .

10. The _____ was flooded when the washing machine pipes broke.

11. The tide took us _____ out to sea in our tiny canoe.

12. The _____ climber dragged herself back up the steep slope.

13. The bridge must be made from concrete or it will _____ .

14. We looked into the tunnel but couldn't see anything in the _____ .

15. I _____ the height of my chair so that I could reach the table.

16. Many people say that the old mansion on the hill is _____ .

Unit 10

Definitions—match the words in the bold with their meanings below

appear	**oncoming**	**predator**	**wingspan**
hatch	**markings**	**claim**	**blurry**
secretly	**refused**	**unable**	**generous**
similar	**let loose**	**fearless**	**innocent**

1. done without others knowing _____
2. not having what it takes to do something _____
3. moving directly towards or at you _____
4. almost but not exactly the same _____
5. to say that something is true even though you can't prove it _____
6. to come into sight _____
7. free from doing anything wrong _____
8. a pattern on the body of an animal _____
9. not at all scared or worried about what might happen _____
10. when an egg opens and produces a baby animal _____
11. a hunter that kills and eats other animals _____
12. set free to do what you want in a place _____
13. cannot be seen or remembered clearly _____
14. said that you will not do something _____
15. willing to give time, money or help to others _____
16. the distance between the tips of the wings _____

Unit 10

Word usage—complete the sentences using the words in bold from the previous page

1. He had not stolen anything from the shop; he was completely _____.

2. These jellies are different in colour but they have a _____ flavour.

3. She is not very _____ because she never buys me a birthday gift.

4. The winner of the competition was _____ in the shop to grab as many toys as possible in three minutes.

5. A fresh water crocodile is a fierce _____.

6. We waited for the ship to _____ on the horizon.

7. The driver of the _____ car had to swerve suddenly to avoid a crash.

8. The _____ of the Boeing 747 aircraft is sixty metres.

9. Why do you _____ that I took your wallet?

10. The eggs will not _____ unless they are kept warm.

11. The brave knight was _____ on the battlefield.

12. Did you see the butterfly with the beautiful violet and green _____?

13. The bully demanded my lunch but I _____.

14. I think I may need glasses because the words in my book are _____.

15. The teacher was _____ to help me during my test.

16. We _____ planned a surprise birthday party for my father.

© MR STEGGELS ADVANCED INSTRUCTION PTY LTD

Test 1

1. Choose the group of words that are **nouns**

   A   hardly, truly, secretly
   B   servant, laundry, energy
   C   swap, fetch, weren't
   D   blurry, similar, snug

2. Choose the best meaning of the word **admit**

   A   to have an idea of something
   B   took place; had an effect on someone or something
   C   agree with something that is true
   D   feeling bad that you have done something wrong

3. Choose the word that is closest in meaning to **twitch**

   A   sick
   B   jerk
   C   cold
   D   scared

4. Choose the word that is most opposite in meaning to **rotten**

   A   fresh
   B   smelly
   C   bad
   D   plenty

5. Which is the odd word out?

   A   fireplace
   B   anywhere
   C   wingspan
   D   mystery

© MR STEGGELS ADVANCED INSTRUCTION PTY LTD

6. Choose the word that best completes the sentence

    Take a run up and _____ yourself into the air over the sandpit.

    A   treat
    B   launch
    C   collapse
    D   carry

7. The letters in **deganam** can be rearranged to make a word meaning

    A   attempted to give the right answer
    B   thought about or wanted to know about something
    C   in place of something or someone else
    D   arranged or did something; succeeded

8. Which pair of words is closest in meaning?

    A   batteries   energy
    B   oncoming   forward
    C   fault   error
    D   carry   collect

9. Which pair of words is most opposite in meaning?

    A   let loose   control
    B   exciting   interesting
    C   explain   argue
    D   plenty   energy

10. Which word should replace the words in bold in the following sentence?

    Do you play any other games **in addition to** Snap and Go Fish?

    A   instead
    B   besides
    C   either
    D   though

© MR STEGGELS ADVANCED INSTRUCTION PTY LTD

11. Which prefix must be added to **appear** to make its opposite?

    A   un-
    B   anti-
    C   mis-
    D   dis-

12. Which can be worn?

    A   jeans
    B   necklace
    C   uniform
    D   all of the above

13. Which word means **to slope in one direction**?

    A   forward
    B   earn
    C   lean
    D   upside down

14. Choose the word that is most similar in meaning to **swallow**

    A   greedy
    B   gulp
    C   refuse
    D   whole

15. Which word can be added to **load** to make a new compound word?

    A   ever
    B   whole
    C   over
    D   oval

© MR STEGGELS ADVANCED INSTRUCTION PTY LTD

16. Choose the word that best completes the sentence

    We kept arguing and didn't get any _____ work done on our project.

    A   busy
    B   further
    C   different
    D   quiet

17. The letters in **gmenaii** can be rearranged to make a word meaning

    A   to have an idea of something
    B   give something and get something else back
    C   to go get something or someone and bring it back
    D   took place; had an effect on someone or something

18. Which pair of words is most opposite in meaning?

    A   hardly   truly
    B   different   special
    C   favourite   common
    D   fearless   scared

19. Choose the best definition of the word **adjusted**

    A   almost but not exactly the same
    B   changed something slightly to make it fit or work better
    C   not likely to move or break
    D   done in the right way

20. Which word should replace the words in bold in the following sentence?

    I had **only just** stepped foot on the bus before it took off.

    A   secretly
    B   hasty
    C   hardly
    D   properly

Test 2

1. Choose the group of words that are **adjectives**

   A   hardly, truly, secretly
   B   servant, laundry, energy
   C   swap, fetch, weren't
   D   blurry, similar, snug

2. Which word means **something important or unusual that happens**?

   A   happened
   B   surprise
   C   event
   D   mystery

3. Choose the word that is closest in meaning to **answer**

   A   argue
   B   reply
   C   false
   D   guess

4. Choose the word that is most opposite in meaning to **innocent**

   A   generous
   B   injured
   C   fearless
   D   guilty

5. Which is the odd word out?

   A   leader
   B   object
   C   servant
   D   daughter

© MR STEGGELS ADVANCED INSTRUCTION PTY LTD

6. Choose the word that best completes the sentence

   We _____ just as the dolphins were performing their aerial tricks.

   A   arrived
   B   howled
   C   discovered
   D   pleased

7. The letters in **bthuorg** can be rearranged to make a word meaning

   A   something not expected
   B   took or carried something or someone to a place
   C   notice, think about or are interested in
   D   instead of; you prefer one thing to another

8. Which pair of words is closest in meaning?

   A   properly   correctly
   B   properly   truly
   C   secretly   guilty
   D   hardly   hasty

9. Which pair of words is most opposite in meaning?

   A   underneath   upside down
   B   upright   upside down
   C   upright   underneath
   D   realised   wondered

10. Which word should replace the words in bold in the following sentence?

    The phone calls between the suspects were recorded **without others knowing**.

    A   properly
    B   truly
    C   correctly
    D   secretly

© MR STEGGELS ADVANCED INSTRUCTION PTY LTD

11. Choose the best word to complete the sentence

The computer _____ finds typing errors and corrects them.

   A   paragraph
   B   sentence
   C   program
   D   servant

12. To show anger, sometimes a young child will

   A   giggle
   B   grin
   C   worry
   D   stomp

13. Which word means **to make something easy to understand**?

   A   argue
   B   describe
   C   explain
   D   program

14. Choose the word that is most similar in meaning to **fetch**

   A   collect
   B   carry
   C   invite
   D   dare

15. Choose the best definition of **rather**

   A   in place of something or someone else
   B   instead of; you prefer one thing to another
   C   used to show that you are honest in what you are saying
   D   at any time, since that time, in the same way as always

© MR STEGGELS ADVANCED INSTRUCTION PTY LTD

16. Choose the words that best complete the sentence

   I _____ to attract the _____ of the teacher by raising my hand.

   A   guessed   attention
   B   managed   grin
   C   howled   markings
   D   managed   attention

17. The letters in **onugerse** can be rearranged to make a word meaning

   A   cannot be seen or remembered clearly
   B   willing to give time, money or help to others
   C   the power you have for doing things that need effort
   D   wanting more money, power, food, things than you need

18. Which pair of words is most opposite in meaning?

   A   hasty   patient
   B   strike   swap
   C   hinge   secure
   D   refuse   trick

19. Choose the best definition of the word **claim**

   A   to come into sight
   B   free from doing anything wrong
   C   not having what it takes to do something
   D   to say that something is true even though you can't prove it

20. Which word should replace the words in bold in the following sentence?

   This material is **almost but not exactly the same** to silk, but much cheaper.

   A   common
   B   identical
   C   similar
   D   beautiful

© MR STEGGELS ADVANCED INSTRUCTION PTY LTD

Test 3

1. Choose the group of words that are **verbs**

   A   hardly, truly, secretly
   B   servant, laundry, energy
   C   swap, fetch, weren't
   D   blurry, similar, snug

2. Choose the best meaning of the word **another**

   A   one more person or thing or amount
   B   one more time
   C   something more, added to what is normal
   D   complete; altogether

3. Choose the word that is closest in meaning to **favourite**

   A   different
   B   special
   C   common
   D   exciting

4. Choose the word that is most opposite in meaning to **pause**

   A   stop
   B   continue
   C   break
   D   again

5. Which can be sweet or savoury?

   A   badge
   B   bruise
   C   picnic
   D   biscuit

© MR STEGGELS ADVANCED INSTRUCTION PTY LTD

6. Choose the words that best complete the sentence

   A _____ does not always have to _____.

A	servant	collapse
B	poem	rhyme
C	leader	worry
D	character	whisper

7. The letters in **harapprag** can be rearranged to make a word meaning

   A   to say or write what something or someone is like
   B   a short piece of writing with at least one sentence that begins on a new line
   C   having the same last sound; a short poem for children
   D   a group of words that starts with a capital letter

8. Which word should replace the words in bold in the following sentence?

   I checked that the screws were tight and that the cart was **not likely to break apart**.

   A   secure
   B   adjusted
   C   interesting
   D   snug

9. Choose the best words to complete the sentence

   _____ anyone turned up to the _____ event.

A	Hardly	special
B	Either	surprise
C	Though	hasty
D	Not	special

10. Which word should replace the words in bold in the following sentence?

    The photographs had been taken from a distance so they were quite **hard to see clearly**.

    A   rough
    B   beautiful
    C   blurry
    D   exciting

11. When **gloom** is changed into a describing word, it becomes

    A   gloomful
    B   glooming
    C   gloomible
    D   gloomy

12. Which means the same as **trick**?

    A   joke
    B   fool
    C   cheat
    D   all of the above

13. Choose the words that best complete the sentence

    I _____ a spelling _____ in the _____.

    A   realised   error   program
    B   adjusted   fault   poem
    C   discovered   error   poem
    D   refused   fault   program

14. A **dare** can be something

    A   silly
    B   embarrassing
    C   dangerous
    D   all of the above

15. **A day in a month and a year** is called

    A   a surprise
    B   a date
    C   an event
    D   an invite

© MR STEGGELS ADVANCED INSTRUCTION PTY LTD

16. Choose the words that best complete the sentence

    _____ returning to camp, we decided to _____ and set up our tents.

    A   Besides   pause
    B   Instead of   unpack
    C   Though   carry
    D   Again   collect

17. The letters in **aerrotpd** can be rearranged to make a word meaning

    A   the person in charge of a group
    B   a female child
    C   someone whose job is to cook, clean or do other work
    D   a hunter that kills and eats other animals

18. Which pair of words is most opposite in meaning?

    A   whisper   howl
    B   howl   quiet
    C   argue   whisper
    D   quiet   haunt

19. Choose the best definition of the word **wondered**

    A   not ordinary or usual
    B   had an idea of something
    C   attempted to give the right answer
    D   thought about or wanted to know about something

20. Which word should replace the words in bold in the following sentence?

    I got too close to the machine and it ripped out **a solid chunk** of my hair.

    A   a whole
    B   plenty
    C   a clump
    D   markings

Test 4

1. Choose the group of words that are **adverbs**

    A   hardly, truly, secretly
    B   servant, laundry, energy
    C   swap, fetch, weren't
    D   blurry, similar, snug

2. Choose the best meaning of the word **snug**

    A   very pretty, pleasant, kind
    B   warm, comfortable and protected
    C   more than enough
    D   touched someone lightly

3. Which word is most opposite in meaning to **generous**?

    A   clever
    B   hasty
    C   greedy
    D   rotten

4. Someone who is **tickled** is likely to

    A   strike
    B   huff
    C   reply
    D   giggle

5. Which word means **the bottom part of the foot or shoe that touches the ground**?

    A   sole
    B   heel
    C   toes
    D   ankle

© MR STEGGELS ADVANCED INSTRUCTION PTY LTD

6. Another word for **gloom** is

   A   ghost
   B   darkness
   C   mist
   D   shadow

7. The letters in **icgmnono** can be rearranged to make a word meaning

   A   to come into sight
   B   the distance between the ends of the wings
   C   moving towards you
   D   a pattern on the body of an animal

8. Which word should replace the words in bold in the following sentence?

   The wolf looked up at the moon and **made a long, loud, sad sound**.

   A   gulped
   B   let loose
   C   howled
   D   none of the above

9. Choose the best words to complete the sentence

   The _____ waited patiently for the eggs to _____.

   A   servant   appear
   B   predator   hatch
   C   manager   bruise
   D   daughter   load

10. Which word should replace the words in bold in the following sentence?

    I tiptoed downstairs to **take a secret, quick look** at the birthday cake.

    A   peep
    B   launch
    C   dare
    D   treat

© MR STEGGELS ADVANCED INSTRUCTION PTY LTD

11. Choose the words that best complete the sentence

The _____ broke off the _____.

A	handle	machine
B	title	necklace
C	object	mountain
D	clump	biscuit

12. Another word for **energy** is

- A hydrogen
- B electricity
- C effort
- D power

13. Choose the words that best complete the sentence

The detective _____ who was _____ of stealing the _____.

A	realised	caught	mystery
B	wondered	guilty	necklace
C	guessed	scared	necklace
D	caught	trembling	necklace

14. Someone who is **famous** is

- A clever
- B fearless
- C well known
- D very pretty

15. Which of the following has to do with **liquid**?

- A leak
- B mountain
- C germs
- D plastic

© MR STEGGELS ADVANCED INSTRUCTION PTY LTD

16. Choose the words that best complete the sentence

    The _____ had to clean the sooty _____ .

A	machine	laundry
B	patient	jeans
C	character	island
D	servant	fireplace

17. The letters in **kramngis** can be rearranged to make a word meaning

    A   a reward; a special experience
    B   to send a new ship into the water or a spacecraft into space
    C   a pattern on the body of an animal
    D   to shake slightly due to feeling cold, sick or scared

18. Choose the word most similar in meaning to **twitching**

    A   collapsing
    B   trembling
    C   interesting
    D   whispering

19. Choose the word most opposite in meaning to **underneath**

    A   below
    B   above
    C   upside down
    D   upright

20. Sport is best played on

    A   a mountain
    B   an island
    C   a picnic
    D   an oval

© MR STEGGELS ADVANCED INSTRUCTION PTY LTD

Test 5

1. Which word means **to feel nervous and upset**?

   A worry
   B twitch
   C tremble
   D scared

2. Choose the best meaning of the word **guilty**

   A feeling bad that you have done something wrong
   B a mistake
   C something not expected
   D something strange that cannot be explained

3. The **person in charge of a group** is called a

   A servant
   B manager
   C leader
   D predator

4. An **annoying person** is sometimes called

   A rough
   B different
   C common
   D a pest

5. The letters in **eodverscid** can be rearranged to make a word meaning

   A found
   B frightened
   C liked best
   D agreed

© MR STEGGELS ADVANCED INSTRUCTION PTY LTD

6. Choose the words that best complete the sentence

   At night, we had to be _____ and could only _____.

A	rough	argue
B	quiet	whisper
C	hasty	worry
D	exciting	appear

7. The letters in **yalrudn** can be rearranged to make a word meaning

   A   a place in a room where a fire burns
   B   a mark where the skin is darker in colour
   C   a place to wash dirty clothes
   D   a small piece of metal worn to show who you are or to which group you belong

8. A **mystery**

   A   is in the direction that is in front of you
   B   is something strange that cannot be explained
   C   describes a place where ghosts keep appearing
   D   involves asking someone to do something silly, embarrassing or that is dangerous

9. Choose the best word to complete the sentence

   _____ you let me come with you, or I will tell Mum where you are going.

   A   Either
   B   Instead
   C   Besides
   D   Though

10. Something that is **false** is

    A   done in the right way
    B   not true
    C   a mistake
    D   none of the above

© MR STEGGELS ADVANCED INSTRUCTION PTY LTD

11. Which letters must be placed at the beginning of **able** to make its opposite

    A   in-
    B   mis-
    C   un-
    D   ill-

12. Choose the words that best complete the sentence

    I had to _____ the _____ in one _____.

    A   unpack   picnic   whole
    B   handle   arrow   load
    C   describe   character   sentence
    D   invite   daughter   date

13. Which word means **pieces of metal that attach a door to the doorframe**?

    A   knots
    B   badges
    C   batteries
    D   hinges

14. Which word is closest in meaning to **complete**?

    A   whole
    B   bare
    C   collapse
    D   earn

15. Another word for **swap** is

    A   fetch
    B   carry
    C   trade
    D   surprise

© MR STEGGELS ADVANCED INSTRUCTION PTY LTD

16. Choose the words that best complete the following sentence

When she was _____ a _____, she went off in a _____.

A	injured	badge	tour
B	scared	predator	mystery
C	refused	treat	huff
D	refused	biscuit	picnic

17. The letters in **rroadwf** can be rearranged to make a word meaning

A   a special set of clothes worn by people who belong to a group
B   wide smile
C   a piece of writing on separate lines sometimes ending with words that rhyme
D   in the direction that is in front of you

18. Something that has **strength and support** will not

A   leak
B   collapse
C   twitch
D   bruise

19. Choose the word that best completes the following sentence

I searched for my keys but couldn't find them _____.

A   ever
B   again
C   anywhere
D   unable

20. Which word means **held on tightly**?

A   hardly
B   truly
C   clump
D   clung

© MR STEGGELS ADVANCED INSTRUCTION PTY LTD

Solutions

Unit 1

Definitions

1	servant	5	unpack	9	greedy	13	adverb
2	mountain	6	energy	10	leak	14	adjective
3	fireplace	7	during	11	verb	15	exciting
4	worry	8	noun	12	plenty	16	famous

Word usage

1	noun	5	servant	9	unpack	13	mountain
2	plenty	6	famous	10	fireplace	14	adjective
3	verb	7	adverb	11	worry	15	energy
4	during	8	greedy	12	leak	16	exciting

Unit 2

Definitions

1	rhyme	5	batteries	9	clever	13	sentence
2	peep	6	busy	10	extra	14	beautiful
3	describe	7	paragraph	11	whole	15	correctly
4	snug	8	handle	12	machine	16	character

Word usage

1	extra	5	busy	9	beautiful	13	describe
2	whole	6	rhyme	10	sentence	14	correctly
3	handle	7	peep	11	snug	15	paragraph
4	clever	8	character	12	batteries	16	machine

Unit 3

Definitions

1	special	5	collect	9	upright	13	common
2	island	6	strike	10	whisper	14	germs
3	discovered	7	underneath	11	different	15	carry
4	scared	8	interesting	12	control	16	favourite

Unit 3

Word usage

1	interesting	5	scared	9	upright	13	different
2	discovered	6	underneath	10	special	14	favourite
3	carry	7	control	11	collect	15	whisper
4	common	8	island	12	strike	16	germs

Unit 4

Definitions

1	fetch	5	trick	9	oval	13	admit
2	swap	6	happened	10	upside down	14	bruise
3	plastic	7	either	11	giggle	15	tickled
4	imagine	8	date	12	object	16	huff

Word usage

1	date	5	either	9	giggle	13	huff
2	upside down	6	plastic	10	swap	14	bruise
3	fetch	7	oval	11	admit	15	tickle
4	object	8	imagine	12	happened	16	trick

Unit 5

Definitions

1	argue	5	caught	9	weren't	13	error
2	false	6	explain	10	load	14	program
3	though	7	patient	11	anywhere	15	pleased
4	reply	8	properly	12	arrow	16	event

Word usage

1	patient	5	event	9	weren't	13	caught
2	argue	6	false	10	load	14	pleased
3	program	7	error	11	though	15	reply
4	properly	8	explain	12	anywhere	16	arrow

© MR STEGGELS ADVANCED INSTRUCTION PTY LTD

Unit 6

Definitions

1	fault	5	guilty	9	invite	13	brought
2	uniform	6	quiet	10	surprise	14	biscuit
3	rather	7	poem	11	grin	15	badge
4	clump	8	another	12	daughter	16	attention

Word usage

1	another	5	fault	9	invite	13	badge
2	uniform	6	clump	10	guilty	14	surprise
3	poem	7	quiet	11	daughter	15	attention
4	rather	8	grin	12	brought	16	biscuit

Unit 7

Definitions

1	necklace	5	instead	9	leader	13	mystery
2	pest	6	earn	10	title	14	forward
3	guessed	7	managed	11	lean	15	copied
4	besides	8	truly	12	wondered	16	hardly

Word usage

1	leader	5	pest	9	copied	13	wondered
2	instead	6	guessed	10	earn	14	besides
3	managed	7	hardly	11	forward	15	title
4	lean	8	mystery	12	necklace	16	truly

Unit 8

Definitions

1	trembling	5	bare	9	sole	13	arrived
2	treat	6	clung	10	rough	14	ever
3	realised	7	picnic	11	gulp	15	pause
4	rotten	8	again	12	stomp	16	jeans

© MR STEGGELS ADVANCED INSTRUCTION PTY LTD

Unit 8

Word usage

1	realised	5	pause	9	gulp	13	clung
2	bare	6	rough	10	stomp	14	sole
3	arrived	7	ever	11	trembling	15	again
4	picnic	8	treat	12	jeans	16	rotten

Unit 9

Definitions

1	hinges	5	hasty	9	howled	13	secure
2	knot	6	adjusted	10	tour	14	dare
3	further	7	twitch	11	gloom	15	injured
4	launch	8	laundry	12	haunted	16	collapse

Word usage

1	howled	5	secure	9	twitch	13	collapse
2	tour	6	knot	10	laundry	14	gloom
3	hasty	7	dare	11	further	15	adjusted
4	hinges	8	launch	12	injured	16	haunted

Unit 10

Definitions

1	secretly	5	claim	9	fearless	13	blurry
2	unable	6	appear	10	hatch	14	refused
3	oncoming	7	innocent	11	predator	15	generous
4	similar	8	markings	12	let loose	16	wingspan

Word usage

1	innocent	5	predator	9	claim	13	refused
2	similar	6	appear	10	hatch	14	blurry
3	generous	7	oncoming	11	fearless	15	unable
4	let loose	8	wingspan	12	markings	16	secretly

Test 1 solutions

Q	A	Notes
1	B	a **noun** refers to a person, place or thing: servant, laundry, energy
2	C	**admit** means agree with something that is true
3	B	**twitch** means to shake suddenly
4	A	**rotten** means smelly, very bad, not fresh
5	D	A, B and C are compound words (fire/place, wing/span, any/where); **mystery** is not
6	B	Take a run up and **launch** yourself into the air over the sandpit.
7	D	**deganam → managed** arranged or did something; succeeded
8	C	**fault** and **error** both mean mistake
9	A	**let loose** means set free to do what you want in a place; **control** means order, limit or rule people or actions
10	B	Do you play any other games **besides** *Snap* and *Go Fish*?
11	D	the opposite of appear is **disappear**
12	D	A, B and C are all clothing or accessories that can be worn
13	C	**lean** means to rest against; slope in one direction.
14	B	**gulp** means to **swallow** a large amount or breathe in air quickly
15	C	**overload** means to add too many things to a load
16	B	We kept arguing and didn't get any **further** work done on our project.
17	A	**gmenaii → imagine** to have an idea of something
18	D	**fearless** means **not at all scared** or worried about what might happen
19	B	**adjusted** means changed something slightly to make it fit or work better
20	C	I had **hardly** stepped foot on the bus before it took off.

Test 2 solutions

Q	A	Notes
1	D	an **adjective** adds more information to a noun; **blurry** photo, **similar** children, **snug** fit
2	C	an **event** is something important or unusual that happens; a **surprise** is unexpected
3	B	**reply** means to answer
4	D	**innocent** means free from doing anything wrong → the opposite is **guilty**
5	B	A, C and D are all things that people can be
6	A	We **arrived** just as the dolphins were performing their aerial tricks.
7	B	**bthuorg** → **brought** took or carried something or someone to a place
8	A	**properly** and **correctly** both mean done in the right way
9	B	**upright** and **upside down** are opposites
10	D	The phone calls between the suspects were recorded **secretly**.
11	C	The computer **program** finds typing errors and corrects them.
12	D	**stomp** means to walk with heavy steps especially when you are annoyed
13	C	**explain** means to make something easy to understand
14	A	**fetch** means to go get something or someone and bring it back → **collect** it
15	B	**rather** means instead of; you prefer one thing to another
16	D	I **managed** to attract the **attention** of the teacher by raising my hand.
17	B	**onugerse** → **generous** willing to give time, money or help to others
18	A	**hasty** means done in a hurry and **patient** means waiting without complaining
19	D	**claim** means to say that something is true even though you can't prove it
20	C	This material is **similar** to silk, but much cheaper.

Test 3 solutions

Q	A	Notes
1	C	a **verb** refers to doing, being or having: swap, fetch, weren't
2	A	**another** means one more person or thing or amount
3	B	**favourite** means liked best of most enjoyed → something that is **special**
4	B	**pause** means stop for a short period of time; **continue** means to keep going
5	D	a **biscuit** is a small, flat disc of dry food that can be **sweet** or **savoury**
6	B	A **poem** does not always have to **rhyme**.
7	B	**harapprag** → **paragraph** a group of words that starts with a capital letter
8	A	I checked that the screws were tight and that the cart was **secure**.
9	A	**Hardly** anyone turned up to the **special** event.
10	C	The photographs had been taken from a distance so they were quite **blurry**.
11	D	**gloom** becomes **gloomy**
12	D	a **trick** is a joke that fools or **cheats** someone; to **fool** or play a **joke** on someone
13	C	I **discovered** a spelling **error** in the **poem**.
14	D	**dare** to ask someone to do something **silly**, **embarrassing** or that is **dangerous**
15	B	a day in a month or a year is called a **date**
16	B	**Instead of** returning to camp, we decided to **unpack** and set up our tents.
17	D	**aerrotpd** → **predator** a hunter that kills and eats other animals
18	A	**whisper** means to speak very softly; **howl** means to make a long, loud, sad sound
19	D	**wondered** means thought about or wanted to know about something
20	C	I got too close to the machine and it ripped out **a clump** of my hair.

Test 4 solutions

Q	A	Notes
1	A	**adverbs** add more information to verbs: hardly, truly, secretly
2	B	**snug** means warm, comfortable and protected
3	C	**generous** means willing to give time, money or help to others **greedy** means wanting more money, power, food, things than you need
4	D	Someone who is **tickled** (touched lightly) is likely to **giggle (laugh)**
5	A	the **sole** is the bottom part of the foot or shoe that touches the ground
6	B	**gloom** is darkness that makes it difficult to see
7	C	**icgmnono** → **oncoming** moving towards you
8	C	The wolf looked up at the moon and **howled**.
9	B	The **predator** waited patiently for the eggs to **hatch**.
10	A	I tiptoed downstairs to **peep** at the birthday cake.
11	A	The **handle** broke off the **machine**.
12	D	**energy** is the **power** you have for doing things
13	B	The detective **wondered** who was **guilty** of stealing the **necklace**.
14	C	**famous** means someone or something that is very well-known
15	A	a **leak** is water or **liquid** flowing out of a container
16	D	The **servant** had to clean the sooty **fireplace**.
17	C	**kramngis** → **markings** a pattern on the body of an animal
18	B	**twitching** a sudden, jerky movement **trembling** a shaking movement due to fear, cold or being upset
19	B	**underneath** means **below** which is opposite to **above**
20	D	an **oval** is an area on which sport is played

© MR STEGGELS ADVANCED INSTRUCTION PTY LTD

Test 5 solutions

Q	A	Notes
1	A	**worry** means to feel nervous and upset
2	A	**guilty** means feeling bad that you have done something wrong
3	C	A **leader** is the person in charge of a group
4	D	A **pest** is an annoying person
5	A	**eodverscid → discovered** found
6	B	At night, we had to be **quiet** and could only **whisper**.
7	C	**yalrudn → laundry** a place to wash dirty clothes
8	B	a **mystery** is something strange that cannot be explained
9	A	**Either** you let me come with you, or I will tell Mum where you are going.
10	B	something that is **false** is not true
11	C	The opposite of **able** is **unable**
12	C	I had to **describe** the **character** in one **sentence**.
13	D	**hinges** are pieces of metal that attach a door to the door frame
14	A	**whole** means complete; altogether
15	C	**swap** means to give something and get something else back; **trade**
16	C	When she was **refused** a **treat** she went off in a **huff**.
17	D	**rroadwf → foward** in the direction that is in front of you
18	B	**collapse** means to fall down suddenly after losing **strength** or **support**
19	C	I searched for my keys but couldn't find them **anywhere**.
20	D	**clung** means held onto something tightly

© MR STEGGELS ADVANCED INSTRUCTION PTY LTD

www.ingramcontent.com/pod-product-compliance
Lightning Source LLC
LaVergne TN
LVHW061318060426
835507LV00019B/2212